Gandy Dancing on The Second Floor

A Collection of Poetry and Short Stories

Cher Duncombe

Cher Duncombe

"Gandy Dancing On The Second Floor," Copyright 2014, by Cher Duncombe. All rights reserved. Printed in the United States of America; no part of this book may be used or reproduced in any manner whatsoever without written permission, except in the case of brief quotations embodied in critical articles and reviews.

First Printing 2014

St Lucie, Fl

Cover Design by Cher Duncombe
Art and Photo Credit Cher Duncombe
Copyright ©2014 Cher Duncombe

ISBN-13:978-1503224728
ISBN 10 1503224724

Gandy Dancing On The Second FLoor

Dedication

To my husband

Richard

who hugged away the nightmares and showed me abiding love for the first time in my life. There is no one like him.

Acknowledgments

This book would not have been compiled and published if not for Mac McGovern. He encouraged me out of my subliminal shell to share these words that were born over many years of late-night writing. Mac's patience with me during the editing process has earned him my deep respect and appreciation.

I also thank my friend MZ, who pushed me for years to write, then write some more. When I was a petulant student, he remained undaunted in his belief in me and in my work. He is a forever friend, one of those very few we find in life.

Gandy Dancing On The Second FLoor

Blurred Lines

Cher Duncombe

Preface

I like my life to run smoothly with as few unexpected twists and turns as possible. I keep the tracks of my life fairly straight with little deviation from what have become norms for me. It was not always like that. Part of getting older is accepting yourself as you are. If you have not reached self-acceptance by now, you may be in for rough times because life can be unlovely. In my mind I live on the second floor of my existence, looking back with some nostalgia at my past, and alternately cringing or cheering at various life-expeditions I have taken. I'm in the world but not part of it in many ways. This gives me a certain sense of empowerment that flies in the face of my age.

I used to call myself "shy" and perhaps that was accurate. The truth lingers somewhere among canards like living on the fringe, doing my own thing, feeling too vulnerable, survival of the fittest, hiding in plain sight, a square peg in a round hole, or feeling unlovely. All these phrases are both apt and contradictory. At this stage in my life, I really don't care. I am a product of my experiences. I have lived a full life in the some of the best, worst, and most dramatic of times. I have been wretchedly close to insanity. I have loved deeply and lost. I have laughed raucously and often at inappropriate times. I have had friends I would give my life for, and I have nearly had life sucked out of me by duplicitous and malicious malcontents.

The other side of this is that I lived in times when we felt compelled to rally for perceived righteousness. I fought for Civil Rights, marched for Women's Rights, worked in shelters for the homeless, fought against domestic violence from a front-row seat, and poured life into my children. I also lived during the assassinations of JFK, Bobby and MLK, and have seen streets named for them all over the country. How many of our youth know why the signs read as they do? Sorry for the aside. I allow myself asides, along with fattening desserts.

I lived during a time when nuns interrupted slow dances between couples by telling us to leave room for the Holy Spirit. I knew darn well the Holy Spirit would not approve of what I was feeling as I danced with my first crush, and the nuns seemed mystically intuitive. I was scared to death of them.

If all of this sounds like I am writing my own eulogy, let me tell you that I am not. I live here on the second floor of my mind where I can clearly see past and present. The future is uncertain but I have no fear. I have been gandy dancing for a long time.

John Lennon Knew My Name

"From our ancestors come our names, but from our virtues, our honors." ~Proverb

Life meanders. We take so many paths and roads, and I have often wondered how much import our given name has. When I was preparing for each child I carried within me, I took a long time choosing a name for them. As I look at my children today, each one looks like their name. Some parents give their children the names of great kings or queens. Do these children feel an onus to live up to that name? Alexander and Victoria, for example, are regal names. My own first name had been a bane for me until I went to college.

My parents named me Cheryl, nothing regal or melodic about that, and even worse when people did not pronounce it correctly. It came out sounding like "Shirl." My own father called me "Shirl!" But there I was, stuck with it. I was a shy child who grew into a shy teenager and even as a college freshman, I was shy. To some extent, and only in looking back now, my name probably had a lot to do with that, at least in my mind. Fortunately college changed my fate for a while.

As a freshman, I was put into a dorm room with a total stranger named Carol. She was gregarious, ebullient, and she hated my name! She had known a "Cheryl" in high school and never liked her. So she told me the first day we met in the dorm that my name would be Cheri, and since she seemed to know many people on campus, she introduced me to them all as Cheri. Within a relatively short time, that was quickly shortened by others to the name Cher. And I was so passive, I allowed it to happen. Actually, I welcomed it. Never again, unless in the presence of my father, would I be called "Shirl." Life was getting good. I was nominated for Homecoming Queen; I had several leads in theatre productions, and had my own radio show at the campus station. "What's in a name?" Perception, that's what. And in the years since college, everyone has known me as Cher, except for one dear friend from high school who still calls me "Shirl." I love her, so I forgive her.

Little did I know that the name Cheryl (or Shirl) was not my name at all, at least it was not my first name. I go back to those meandering roads and truly believe that every road has its purpose. Recently, I needed a copy of my Certificate of Baptism from the Roman Catholic Church in which I had been raised. While I knew I had been baptized, I had never seen that certificate.

Since both my parents are deceased, I began the process of obtaining that certificate through proper channels.

Yesterday it arrived. I first looked at the seal to make certain it had been authenticated, and then I almost put it back in the envelope. Turning it over, I saw the name "Julia Cheryl." Hah! My name is Julia, not Cheryl, and certainly not "Shirl." I was, I am, and have been all along, Julia, which was my grandmother's name. Julie, everyone called her Julie and I had adored her. I gasped aloud when I saw this. Why did my parents never tell me? Why did they drop my *real* first name? I had to tell my kids. Family identity crisis here! So at 1:00 a.m. this morning I was texting them, in part, because through the years when they wanted to rile me, they would call me "Shirl." No more of that.

One of my kids texted back, said that was a "lovely name," and sent me a link to the Beatles song, "Julia." My kids grew up listening to the Beatles, especially to *Abbey Road*. This is one song I had never heard, though judging from the number of hits it has received on You Tube, I must be one of the few who didn't know it. All this time I should have known that John Lennon knew my name, even if my parents didn't.

So you can call me Cher. You cannot call me Shirl. You may call me Julia, but I might not turn in recognition yet. Please give your child a name they will like. Today is John Lennon's birthday. I miss him still after all these years, and now I feel a true connection to him. Julia. We both loved that name. From an ancestor came my name. From a man of peace and some virtue, came honor. Happy Birthday, John Lennon. You touched our lives in ways you never knew.

Cher Duncombe

The Wake: In-laws and Outlaws

Most of us have had to face the fact that sometimes our in-laws are not people we would have chosen. They are just part of the lottery ticket you draw when you are born into a family. There is something about funerals, or in my Irish family, Wakes, that bring out the best and worst in a family.

My mother had passed away and the Wake was held in the huge Victorian house I owned at the time. The house was overflowing with people we deemed to be either in-laws or outlaws. My brother had flown in from Atlanta to help and quickly became my leaning post. He set up the bar in my kitchen and bartended throughout the afternoon and into the night, because that's the tradition, you see. That long? Yes, it was that long. Mom had a wealth of friends and even those of her former in-laws who had not seen her in years, attended the Wake. They were taking stock. "Oh my, she really aged." Silent thoughts. I had many silent thoughts. "What investment company did she use," someone asked. I couldn't bring myself to respond to that.

It is part of the Irish tradition to open the doors to your home and welcome all those who wished to pay their respects. Sure 'n it's a bane when you are the one hosting it. There were people at the Wake whose names I could barely recall. Some were members of my father's family. My parents had divorced years before, and Dad's family had never really liked my Mom anyway but they upheld tradition and attended her Wake. "Too highfalutin', that one," I recalled they had said. Memories and unresolved grievances went on like this throughout the Wake. My brother and I were grieving, but still trying to be good hosts. Our nerves were getting frayed. I stayed sober and my brother drank. But he had a *list* on a small notepad inside his suit coat pocket.

My brother would ceremoniously show me The List at discreet intervals. One of my maternal aunts, whom my mother had been certain had stolen money from her, was there. I was gracious and my brother smiled. But he took out his notebook and off he went to the kitchen and straight to the bar. He caught me within a few moments and showed me The List. Then he explained, "These are people we will never see again. Have no contact with them, okay?" I looked up at his 6'2" frame and nodded with complete understanding. He was nothing if not organized. This was to be set in granite, possibly beside Mom's headstone! I was almost ready for a drink but Mom had made certain I knew that decorum was of great importance, especially for women and most especially for me.

Guests came and went and there was singing of old Irish melodies harmonized by the uncles in attendance. Much of this was fun, I must admit. Old Aunt Dottie hiked her skirt to do an Irish jig. I mean, she hiked that skirt so high you had to turn your head. What was she, eighty, maybe? Kudos to her, I thought, but even second cousin twice removed, Aunt Dottie made The List. Inappropriate for our children, my brother determined. I was too tired to argue. This was supposed to be a celebration of our mother's life but in the tradition I had experienced in other Wakes, the in-laws and out-laws were making that difficult.

By the end of the night of food, drink, gossip, and The List, I was exhausted. We were saying our good-byes at the front door to the last of the intruders when I heard I heard my daughter scream, "MMMMMum! My water broke!"

I am going to be cremated and no notices will be printed in the local newspaper. It's on My List.

Cher Duncombe

Characters in My Life Collage: Chops

I grew up in a community with people who drank Martinis, owned small planes, had in-ground swimming pools, their own interior decorators, proffered lavishly catered dinners, never served sandwiches with crust, and seemed to work very hard at being boring. This may account for the fact that once I left home, having been made to parade around the house with five books on my head to learn proper posture, I became enchanted by people who were far different than those in my limited and painfully dull realm.

Many of my friends have been eccentric and probably border-line, or full throttle fringe elements. Some were scholarly, even brilliant. And there were those who showed me aspects of life that made me feel like Alice in her Wonderland. With a nod to John Lennon I say, "In my life, I loved them all."

Chops

I met Chops at a picnic in 1997. Some friends had said they were taking me to a picnic at a small house in the country. It was already hot that early Saturday afternoon, and we drove in a three-car caravan for several hours. Soon the highway became a gravel road, which became a sort of lane that took us deep into the woods. We parked our cars in the midst of a variety of pick-up trucks and more than a few Harleys.

As I got out of the car, I saw so many people that my mind became a Kodak camera. Somehow I knew this was really different. The "small house in the country" was more like a shack with chipped white paint on planks of wood, oranged in spots by rusty nails. There must have been at least fifty people gathered in various places. Some were standing around a dirt pit that had been dug in the ground. Across the pit was some sort of metal rod upon which a pig was being roasted and turned by guys with a can of beer in one hand, while the other hand helped turn the roasting rod. Others were grilling hot dogs and hamburgers and the air smelled delicious. Laughter was bouncing off trees that surrounded this haphazard bucolic setting, and I was handed a beer. No one was formally introduced but we were all talking to one another. I couldn't tell you exactly what the conversations were because like magic, as soon as my beer was empty, another was placed in my hand. Gracious folks, they were!

My friends invited me to sit at a make-shift picnic table and over came this burly guy with a red bandana tied around his head. He had a beard, mutton sideburns (chops) and what could be seen of his face was pockmarked. He was wearing a beater shirt that showed huge arms covered in ink. I heard several of my friends shout, "Hey Chops!" Obviously they knew him. He smiled, then laughed, "Hey yourselves," as he sidled onto the bench. "You gotta go for a ride with Chops on his Hog," they said to me, as though this was a rite of passage. "No, I don't think so, but thanks," I said with a half-laugh and my heart in my mouth. Drinking then driving on a Hog seemed over the top, even for an escapade.

But somehow the beer kept flowing, music was playing, and my friends goaded me for hours about riding with Chops on his Hog before I finally relented. Chops smiled at me and said, "Now don't you be afraid. Old Chops'll take care of you. You just get on behind me and hold on tight." I was getting sober fast. You can take the girl out of the city.... "Wait!" I heard myself say. "Don't you have a helmet?" Chops cocked his head at me, smiled, and then called for somebody to bring him a helmet. Chops fixed the strap so it fit just right under my chin. Now everybody was up on their feet, cheering.

I wrapped my arms around Chops. Well, I couldn't get my arms around Chops, but I did the best I could, and off we went. We were on the gravel road when Chops' bandana flew into the air and down to the ground. He did a semi-turn and said to me, "You gotta grab that for me." Over the roaring engine I screamed, "What! How? I can't!" He slowed the Hog to a crawl and told me to just reach down and pick it up. You would have to see the size of this man to know that you don't argue with him! I managed to scoop up the bandana and we scorched the gravel on the road as Chops revved up. Once we were on the highway, my head was tossed back and the wind felt like soft kisses. Wow, so this is what it's all about! It was glorious, and the sun was beginning to set in beautiful hues. I just soaked it all in.

As we arrived back at the picnic, people stopped what they were doing and came over to Chops and me with hoots and whistles. "This little thing almost broke my ribs, holdin' on so tight," Chops laughed. I sat back down at the picnic table with my friends, old and new. Chops offered to make me a Hobo sandwich. I had no idea what that was, but said, "Sure!" Soon he returned with a slice of bread, crust included, and said that it's just dipped in some hot bacon fat, held over the fire to toast, and he had tossed a few slices of bacon on top. I don't remember having a sandwich that tasted so good.

We sat at the table eating Hobo sandwiches and drinking more beer, when three old men, slight of build with shirts and jeans that just hung on their bodies, came out of the "small house in the country" carrying fiddles. They started playing Bluegrass songs as though they were on a stage in Nashville, and we all got up and danced a jig or two. It was one of the best summer days of my life.

About a year or so later, one of my friends told me that Chops had died. He had crashed his Harley into a pole at Sturgis. No, he wasn't wearing a helmet. Oh Chops. I will never forget him and thoughts of him that summer day will always make me smile. Every time I hear Bluegrass music, I look up to the sky and hope that he is dancing. I have never ridden a Harley since that picnic at a small house in the country.

Gandy Dancing On The Second FLoor

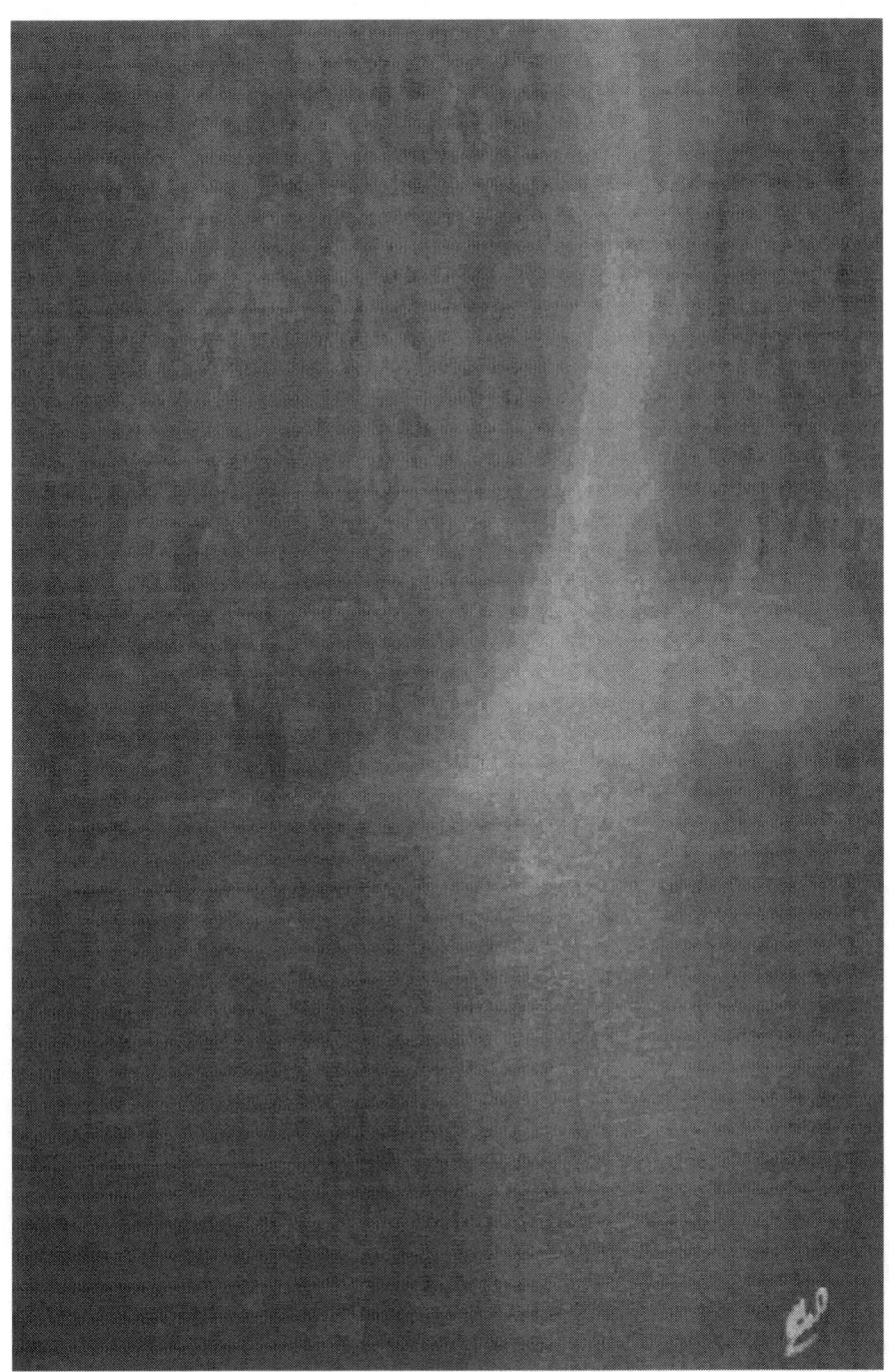

Autumn Reflections

Cher Duncombe

Characters in My Life Collage: The Sparrow

Most families have their heroes or heroines, those whom the family deems as destined for greatness. In my family, The One was a second cousin named Patricia. She was part of the extended Irish side of my family, and I had adored her when we were growing up. Patricia was ten years older than I. She had beauty and grace, a looming contrast to my adolescent awkwardness, and had already done quite a few prestigious modeling jobs. She was fragile looking, like a porcelain doll. Her large, warm brown eyes gazed at you softly and she spoke with gentility and an openness that quietly glimpsed a loving, tender, and vulnerable heart.

As often happens with friends and family, time and distance take their separating tolls, and I did not see Patricia for a long time. One day some years ago, I left my office in the city for lunch on a frigidly cold day and fighting against slapping cold winds. The sidewalks were crowded with noon-ers in their usual hurried manner. Suddenly, I caught sight of a beautiful woman dressed in a stunning fur coat standing across the street from me. She was stopping people at random trying to communicate with them in a seemingly desperate and urgent manner. I observed the brusque treatment she was receiving.

Since I was a social worker at the time, I knew this was not a safe thing for a woman to do, especially in the city and most especially for hungry people eager to escape the confines of their office. Pondering this and still watching her, a jolt of reality struck. Suddenly I realized that it was Patricia! I dodged traffic and slush in the street and ran to her. She recognized me immediately. We hugged and said the Oh My's and How Are You's and It's Been So Long's, almost like the Rosary.

On that street corner Patricia began telling me she had received an epiphany from the Blessed Mother that the world was going to end soon. Was I ready? I was befuddled, taken off guard and it was noisy. Where was the model I had known? I couldn't quite catch what she was rapidly saying, so I suggested we go inside a nearby restaurant for coffee. "Oh no," she said, "I'm not allowed in there." A flash of my Irish got the best of me and I responded, "Oh yes you are!"

We entered a restaurant I frequented and a waitress arched her eyebrow at Patricia. I arched an eyebrow back and told her she was with me. It was all so surreal. After all, this was The One! Don't you know that?

Reluctantly and with a hint of "humph," the waitress seated us. I ordered coffee for me and tea for Patricia. She talked; I listened.

She said the Blessed Mother had told her of a coming apocalypse and that she was to warn people. Though she told me that she was married to an architect and had a beautiful home in the suburbs, she said she rode buses all over the city day and night, committed to heeding the Blessed Mother's request that she foretell this event. Patricia told me almost casually that she had been beaten several times and once her leg had been broken. I cringed at the thought of anyone hurting this fragile, if tormented soul. I tried to dissuade her from riding these buses and from approaching strangers but she would have none of it. With solemn and quiet resignation, she said that in her epiphany she had been told she was to die the death of a martyr. It was all too much for my psyche to absorb.

That was the last time I saw Patricia. For a while the Pittsburgh Post-Gazette did some articles about her and dubbed her "The Sparrow." The Sparrow Christian Symbol represents and symbolizes the concern of God for the most insignificant living things. I could understand why they did articles about Patricia. She was a fascinating anomaly, lovely, delicate, and beautifully dressed, but undaunted in what she saw as her spiritual, albeit dangerous, calling. Then she disappeared. To this day no one knows what actually happened to her.

After our meeting near my office, I had contacted some family members. Some tried to label her in terms other than crossed synapses. "She had problems," they would say euphemistically. But did she? I suppose only God knows. Her family was left in earthly limbo, a sorrowful place to be. My prayer is that Patricia, this sweet and gentle child of God, is at rest in His arms and that His eye is on "The Sparrow."

Cher Duncombe

Characters In My Life Collage: The Radical Priest

Absolution. I knew I needed it, but I had this attraction, you see. Should I turn left or right? The glory of heaven or the pains of hell? It all started at a school board meeting. I was a single mom, having left an bad marriage and taking my four young children with me. I was still in recovery. And I was angry. How could a man have been so cruel? It would be a long time until I sorted through it all. In the meantime, I had these kids to raise.

We lived in a small house in a small community, but the house was on a busy road, one that seemed to beg people to drive fast, even though several families had children who walked that road to and from school. There were no speed limit signs along the stretch that our children walked. After several near misses of cars almost hitting my kids, I got together with other parents in the vicinity. We were all concerned and I was outraged, the anger in me over a multitude of issues still simmering beneath the surface. That is why they elected me to represent them at a school board meeting to try to have this speeding situation resolved. They liked my anger and feistiness.

The night of the school board meeting, the other parents were there, but I was the spokesperson. I stood to make our case, but when the board members seemed dismissive, I got louder, ranting and raving that they would have the blood of our children on their hands. They threw me out of the meeting!

I was standing in the parking lot by my car, and I was still steaming. That's when he appeared. This handsome middle-aged priest with his collar, blue eyes and white-too-soon hair came over to me. He was gorgeous, not to mention off-limits. He laughed a quiet laugh in a velvet voice and said, "You kinda lost it in there." It turned out that after I had been thrown out of the meeting, he had risen to my defense and was told to leave as well. I laughed as he told me the story. We talked for a long time under the glow of streetlights and he learned my story. "The best way to get rid of your anger is to help others, "he said. Then he asked me to do some volunteer work at a homeless shelter he ran in the community. I agreed and the next day I was there serving lunch to the homeless and castaways. It was a healing process. Father O'Riley had been right.

As the months went by, I became more and more involved with the shelter and soon Father O'Riley put me on the Board of Directors. He was truly a radical priest, refusing any government funds for this project and shunning any possible intervention by powers that be. We had a lot of meetings, he and I, and there was a glimmer in his eye every time we spoke. He would sometimes take my hand or put his arm around my shoulder. He peered into my eyes as a man, not a priest. But feelings were there, no doubt about it. I wrestled with these feelings, both as a Catholic who had almost joined the convent, and as a woman. Women know the signs, even if we don't act upon them. Oh, but I wanted to act. He had me in my mind, and that is how a man first gets a woman, in her mind. Priest or not, he let his attraction to me be known. There were times when we were together that I thought I heard Hal from 2001: A Space Odyssey saying, "Alert! Alert here! Sin about to be committed!" So I prayed.

God must have heard me because I soon received a job offer with a good salary and would move from that community. The hours at the board meetings ended, and so did my time with Father O'Riley. We kept in touch by phone and once in a while, I would read a newspaper article about him, always stirring the pot of politics in that community he loved.

Several years later, my Mom passed away. Though she had become a Catholic to please my father, she had never gone to Mass, nor had she been affiliated with any church. I called Father O'Riley and asked if he would preside over her funeral. Always accommodating, he said he would. After the services, I held a Wake at my house, which was brimming with people. My brother was tending bar, and had served Father O'Riley more than a few drinks. At some point, and it's still a bit hazy, this gorgeous radical priest came up behind me, put his arms around me, and sighed into my ear. I could have died and gone to heaven—or hell, had I chosen the wrong door. I just turned and smiled, and held him at arm's length.

Today, some years later, I often think of him and the possibilities of what might have been if I had given into my desires and his. It's fantasy, nothing more. But let me tell you, I could have easily taken a wrong turn and there would have been no absolution for me. I sigh, and turn to other thoughts with my soul still intact.

Cher Duncombe

My Jung Dream

Murder of the Spirit: A Story of Domestic Violence

Preface:

The Commandment says Thou Shalt Not Kill. Do we realize that murder of the spirit is as egregious as murder of the physical body? Statistics show that averages of three women in the United States are murdered each day through an act of domestic violence. It is a closet issue for many and crosses all socio-economic boundaries. I have been there. I know. Having been abused as a child by my father, there was a warped part of me that accepted abuse as the norm. Often women subliminally seek out partners who are like their fathers. It is a sad track that too often ends in murder of the body and spirit. We can free ourselves, but not by ourselves. Still, who wants to admit they are being savagely treated by the very person who is meant to protect them? Many feel they have brought it upon themselves. It is an issue of shame, among other things.

The following is a personal account of some of the domestic violence I experienced in a marriage. As you read it, do not weep for me, but for those women languishing in fear, rejection, and merciless pain, and who are alone in their despair.

There were times in my former marriage when I would bite my arm till it bled while lying next to him. I could not stand the stench of the man who physically and emotionally raped my soul. I would at times seek refuge under the blankets of my bed just to escape his madness which had begun infiltrating my own psyche. At these times, he would fling open the bedroom door and turn on the overhead light, robbing me of my pretense of shutting out the ugly reality of his existence. He would stand over me with arms crossed in blatant bloated power and just stare. I would shudder, not knowing what to expect next. Another beating? Another near-death experience as he choked me? Sometimes he would leave after a few minutes, but he left the glaring light on, almost daring me to turn it off in his perceived power play. I pulled the covers over my head and retreated into an unlit void. Still alive, both of us.

Weeks would go by without him saying a word. Cajoling did no good. Anger made it worse and the silence, I learned, could at any moment turn into roaring violence. It was usually directed at me, but there were times it would be directed at my children. With them he was not physically violent, but his words to them were like baseball bats. I tended to their wounds as best I could when he was not around. They knew little of violence I was experiencing. He made certain there were no witnesses.

He had issued edicts to me saying that if I ever left he would hunt me down and kill not only me, but my children like the thrill of chasing game in hunting season. I believed him. I thoroughly had come to believe that he was all-powerful and most mighty. And what would happen to my children? Consequences weighed on my mind in a continuum. Would they be better off without me, out of the frightening course on which I had unwittingly set our collective paths? Certainly they would be better off without him. Yes, I thought about killing him. In my splintered psyche, I did think about it.

One night when the children were all out of the house involved in various activities, he reached a feverish pitch in his violence. He blocked the doors as I tried to leave. A slap! I went down. A kick! I crawled. Vile words issued like venom spewing from a snake. I ran to the bathroom, locked the door and downed a bottle of his whatever pills. Breaking in the door, he took no notice of the empty bottle on the floor. More pain from him, but my senses were beginning to dull. I crawled to the kitchen and grabbed a knife. No, I would not kill him. Instead, I cut my wrists just so, and the blood poured out of me taking the last bit of my spirit with it.

I awoke in a hospital with several doctors hovering over me. It was all so surreal. What had happened? Where was HE? HE came to see me. Repentant. Crying. I was numb. Later a psychiatrist sat beside my bed. In gentle tones he said, "You didn't really want to kill yourself, did you?" Through tears I tried to answer saying, "No, no, I just, I just..." He finished my sentence, "You just wanted it to stop, didn't you?" At that moment my recovery began. I was put in touch with an agency that aided victims of domestic violence. They helped my ailing psyche reach clarity and poured strength into me through their understanding and kindness. Most of all, they helped me secure a Protection of Abuse order and accompanied me to the hearing. One year. The judge told him he could not come near the children or me for one year. That would buy me time to get out and move on.

It was not an easy road, but it was a positive one. Was there collateral damage? Sure. I had to give up a house and most of my life possessions to start over. I had stayed too long at the fair of wrong-doing. But I salvaged what I could from the wreckage and my life, thanks in large part to Domestic Violence counselors, continues in a healthy way.

Victims of Domestic Violence come in all colors. We are rich; we are poor; we are your neighbors; we are your friends; we are your co-workers, and we are often hidden in the closet of fear. While you may not feel comfortable in approaching someone in this situation, I can only hope that through this personal account you may gain some awareness. The spirit within us all deserves to live without fear and without violence.

Cher Duncombe

Her Beloved Ukraine

I can see her standing over the stove, stirring a pot of her homemade soup. She stood about 5'4" and wore colorfully printed dresses, invariably covered with a heavy white cotton apron. Elastic stockings that looked like Ace bandages were rolled tightly just above the knees; her feet held sturdy by thick-soled black shoes tied with black laces. And there was a deep tone to her voice that belied her natural beauty of white hair, blue eyes, cream-colored skin, and a delicate face with lines of a thousand stories. She was my maternal grandmother who had emigrated here from the Ukraine in 1912. Her name was Julia.

Julia married Dmitro who was also from the Ukraine and had arrived in the States two years prior to Julia. He was a factory worker and she was the caretaker of their family of six children. I have few memories of "Mitro." He died when I was three. I do recall standing outside my grandparent's bedroom door while doctors and nurses huddled around him and took turns raising his arms. I didn't know why they were doing that, but it seemed important and their faces were tense. He passed away that day. A pall spread throughout the house as grief attached itself. That's all I remember about him. But Julia lived to be 91. Being her first grandchild I was blessed to share many days and weeks with her throughout the years. She was the most nurturing person I have ever known. She was not a person of idle conversation. Neither am I. Nature vs nurture?

When she did speak, she spoke with purpose and intent. She read and spoke English very well, but much to my liking, she maintained a thick Ukrainian accent. Julia also maintained many Ukrainian traditions, like melting candle wax in a pot on the stove, dipping toothpicks in it and making intricate designs on Easter eggs before dying them. It was pure art. It was a tradition derived from her long-ago Ukraine. She worked silently. She also had down feathers delivered by truckloads to her garage and with a wheelbarrow she would transport load after load to the basement where here foot-peddle sewing machine sat. Soon Julia had sewn a new down comforter. None of those remain in the family today. Sometimes the importance tradition is lost on those who do not understand that love comes in many forms. I buy down comforters in department stores now. It's just not the same.

Julia read the morning newspaper every day, moistening her fingers to turn the pages with her cup of coffee nearby. One morning while I was staying with her, she read an article about Nikita Khrushchev. This was long before the Cold War ended, and the article had upset her so much that she threw the newspaper across the room and shouted, "Communist!" When I asked her why she was so angry she told me a story.

When she was a young girl in the Ukraine, her family had a farm. Once she had been struck by lightning and her parents put her in hay inside the barn so she could recover. I seldom asked questions. I listened. As she spoke of the farm in her beloved Ukraine, her face became solemn, then fierce looking. Soldiers, she told me, had come to their farm. They tied her parents to trees and set them on fire. They then proceeded to set the entire farm on fire as she watched, hidden in the woods. After telling me the story, she put her face in her hands and cried, "Bozhe, Bozhe, Bozhe." God, God, God.

In the small suburban house her children had purchased for her after Mitro's death, Julia had a patch of a garden. She tended to it every day, pulling errant weeds and letting green onions, carrots, cabbage, squash and tomatoes grow. It seemed her homage to the farm of her family that had been burned so many years ago. She did this in silence, as she did so many things. The lines etched upon her face told many more stories. Does history account for grief that cannot be spoken?

And as I watch news stories today about the tug-of-war happening in my grandmother's beloved Ukraine, I cannot help wondering how many people are putting their faces in their hands, suffering and crying, "Bozhe, Bozhe, Bozhe" once again.

Cher Duncombe

The Gypsy Tea Room

Every time a decision needed to be made, the old lady took a bus to the city. "Where are you going, Muma?" her family would ask. With a dismissive reply as she left the front door she would say, "To see the gypsy!" Off she would go with a sense of urgency, and moving in an awkward gait upon her thick-soled shoes. Her handbag, though worn-looking on the outside, contained some cash in a tapestry pouch, a small notepad, a sharpened pencil, and a Dream Book in case she would also stop at the Brass Rail to play a number. At eighty plus six, and widowed for many years, her guideposts had dwindled. In whom could she seek counsel? Not her sons, who were smart, yes, but not so smart in the ways of fortune-telling and dream interpretations. For those she needed the gypsy.

On one of these forays, she took her young granddaughter. The girl was perhaps five years old, quiet, and somewhat forlorn looking with doe-brown eyes that gazed upon the old lady with loving affection. They sat on the cross-wise seat in the back of the bus where the fumes were noxious, but the old lady could watch everything and everyone with a studious glare, never releasing the child's hand. The old lady's lips were pursed just as tightly as her fingers that clutched the handbag against her bosom.

The bus arrived at Market Square in the city, and the old lady lifted the child's hand to signal departure without speaking. In Market Square, people were either hurried in their pace or stopped at one of the vendors and filling their sacks with breads and fruits and cheese. To the girl the aromas were a welcome replacement of the fumes on the bus, but she had to walk quickly to stay astride the grandmother. Finally they came to a door, the opening of which showed a wooden staircase. After the old lady affixed her hat properly, she held the girl's hand as they began the assent to The Gypsy Tea Room.

At the top of the stairs they entered a room filled with tables covered in white linen cloths and people who spoke in quiet voices. The wooden floor sounded the arrival of each guest as their shoes trod upon cross-grains. Once seated, the old lady ordered sandwiches, one for the girl and one for her. And tea, of course. They had come here for the tea. They ate in silence, the grandmother and the child. The tea tasted bitter to the girl, but the old lady drank it carefully and took notice of the leaves left in the bottom of the cups.

Everything was done in silence between the old lady and the girl, as though a pact of confidence was theirs to keep. Soon she appeared, the gypsy wearing a colorful scarf as her dark hair flowed around her shoulders. She seated herself next to the old lady. They spoke in hushed tones and the gypsy eyed the girl who was a bit frightened and a bit in awe at the same time. The gypsy looked inside both tea cups and at the brownish tea leaves in the bottom of each cup. Finally she spoke.

Leaning into the old lady but looking at the girl, the gypsy said, "This one has the gift." The grandmother breathed in so deeply that the girl was alarmed, and said, "Gramma?" But the old lady shushed her and rocked her body back and forth for several moments. Then from the small tapestry pouch inside her handbag, she paid the gypsy who continued to study the girl. And so it began. They did not go to the Brass Rail that day. They left The Gypsy Tea Room, walked through Market Square and boarded a bus. The fumes were noxious.

Cher Duncombe

The Investigation

We never know where our gifts will take us in life or if, in fact, we will use them. The old lady had been told that her grandchild had a "gift." What that might be was anyone's guess but the old lady told the little girl that she had one. The child had no idea what she was talking about until one day some months later when she was playing outdoors on a summer day and glanced up at the blue sky. She saw a vision. There were three cameo-style images looking at her, Jesus, Mary, and God Himself. She stared for a long time. She was used to seeing planes in the sky but not pictures. She ran inside the house to get her mother so she could see the beautiful pictures that had been painted in the sky. But when the mother came out, they were gone. The mother scoffed and she hurriedly went back inside the house.

The girl, feeling dejected, kicked around some sand in her sandbox, and then sat in the grass, with elbows on her knees and fists at her cheeks. She would not, no, she would not, look at that sky again. But after several moments, she couldn't help herself. She looked up at the sky. The images were there, as clear as any painting or picture she had ever seen. They remained in the sky above her until her mother called her to come inside. That was the last time she would see them.

She never mentioned the vision to anyone again, but the images of those three cameos stayed tucked in a pocket of her mind. Yeah, yeah, I know. Some people don't believe in God, let alone Jesus and the Virgin Mary. But the girl did. And as she grew older, her thought was that this had been a sign from God. Perhaps this was a gift presented to her so she would have courage and faith when life was difficult. Once in a while things would happen; odd things would happen. There would be a moment of such clarity that it was almost startling.

 Sometimes she had a spiritual faith and sometimes she did not. Her life had always vacillated between total euphoria and complete despair. There seemed to be no middle ground for her. Maybe that is why she became an investigator. Well, it was as good a reason as any. She loved putting together pieces of a puzzle that spidered into leads.

She knew as soon as her boss put the manila folder on her desk that this case was...she didn't know, but the word "freaky" came to mind. She settled on "different." Certainly it would be a challenge. She had been asked to find a child. Not much background info was there but enough for a start: mother's name and her last known address in Idaho; father's name and whereabouts unknown. Alrighty then, she said to herself after her boss left, let's start here in Pennsylvania.

She ran a DMV check and came up with a late model truck registered in the father's name some seventy miles away. God, she hated it up there. Klan country. Never knew who or what you would run into. People were hard to find out there in thick country. Many lived on lanes and those lanes were not even marked on maps. A lot of people who lived in that territory did not have mailboxes, opting instead to use a postal box and keeping their whereabouts unknown and hidden. After driving for several hours, she had been about to give up when she drove past a lane with a carved wooden sign that read, "Beer Bullets and Babes." That's the place, she thought. And it was.

No vehicles were in the driveway of this slipshod, red brick, neglected house. She knocked at the door but no one answered. To top it all off like too much foam when someone else pours a beer, there were no houses nearby. Damn it to hell. Miles separated this house from others. So for days she did a stake-out and was hidden by trees and thickets of overgrown shrubs that seemed to crawl along the ground. She would drive there are different times of the day, waiting and eating Pop Tarts in her car. On her third try, she saw the red truck.

She stayed in the car and watched as a man of medium build wearing black-rimmed glasses exited the car. She checked the DMV photo against what she could see of him through binoculars. That's him. Thank God! She was getting tired of this stake-out, especially when she needed to pee. Wait. He had turned back to the truck and was lifting a small little boy down. They went into the house together. Where was the girl she was looking for? She let five minutes go by then moved her car into the driveway.

She had memorized everything she knew about him, which wasn't much. He answered the door when she knocked and in her best ditsy voice and with a broad smile she said, "Hey there, you must be Frank!" He smiled and said, "Yep, I am. What can I do for you?" She responded that she just needed to ask him a few questions about a new program for his child's health care that he might be interested in. He opened the door for her to come in. Bad mistake. She scanned the place fast, taking inventory of the half empty bottles of booze and a nasty smell in the place. Then she did the deed. She showed him her badge.

With that, he kicked the door behind her closed and pinned her against the stove. She was wearing a trench coat, so he couldn't tell if she was carrying or not. She put one hand in her coat pocket and yelled the first thing that came to her mind, "Up against the wall!" She left out mf-er. He did it. Then she said softly and firmly, "Let's talk, Frank, but don't turn around." He stood there against the wall, and in her mind she shouted to herself, "Yes!"

"I'm looking for your daughter, that's all. So help me out here, okay?" He turned his head toward the little boy with short blonde hair and said, "Right there. There she is." She spoke to the child and asked, "What's your name, sweetie?" The boy who turned out to be a girl spoke softly and said, "Caroline." That was the missing girl. Jules had a bad feeling about this. The girl's hair had been cut like a boy's and she was wearing a little boy's outfit.

Frank started to move but she put her free hand against his back and whispered so the child couldn't hear, "Don't move. Do. Not. Move." He stayed against the wall, and with the hand that did not have a gun, she pulled out her cell phone and pushed the programmed button for the State Police. She told them her location as precisely as she could, and she requested they bring

Children's Services with them. She pressed her hand hard against Frank's back. The stench of him wrecked her senses. Putrid.

Within ten minutes the State Police pulled in, along with people from Children's Services. One Officer put a gun on Frank while Jules went outside to explain her investigation to the Sergeant. Turns out that Frank had three outstanding warrants in Idaho for some very bad stuff, like child molestation. He had cut the girl's hair and was about to go on the run again. The child was placed with protective services and ended up living with her maternal grandmother, who was said to be a good woman.

About one month later, Jules was asked to come to Headquarters for a meeting. Unbeknownst to her, the higher-ups were giving her an award for finding Caroline. Jules felt entirely undeserving. As she stood in front of her co-workers and supervisors from Headquarters, photos were taken. She shook hands, even as her legs were shaking. She thought about "the gift," her grandmother, and the gypsy and wondered how she ended up here. Lucky, yes, but why? She went outside, looked up at the sky and thought she saw…something.

Sometimes She Goes to Keening

Late at night and on rare occasions, she awakens to sorrow that cannot be stilled, sublimated nor silenced. She lies in bed listening to the pounding of her heart, willing it to be slowed in tempo. It lies not in her chest, but rather, in her ears. Beating. Beating. Harder. Louder. In her mind, in her mind are thoughts of closed yesterdays that now lie in the forefront of consciousness, taunting her fears, her recriminations, and her laments. Is this what we must face as life leaves us in anguish? Can the deaths of those we've loved ever be reconciled by the living?

And part of her thinks how easy it would be just to let go of life's tether. Suffer no more, for surely this pain cannot sustain existence in this realm. In those moments of anguish and torment, sometimes she goes to keening. It first happened some years ago upon the death of her sibling. People told her she must go on, must stop grieving, must live life to the fullest. But the pain, and yes, it is unmistakably pain, will not cease. Sometimes it abates and sometimes it forces its way out of the cave and against her will.

It is in these moments that she keens. There is a low, soft moan that rises from her throat but not through her closed lips, over and over and over. It is a sound the Irish know. It is a sound she heard at the family's wakes. It is the sound of grief that cannot be enunciated but is understood by the sharing nonetheless. With whom can she share this grief? Only God Himself knows. She rises from her bed and almost glides above the floor until she finds her grandmother's rocking chair. Keening had been done in this very chair when her uncle passed away unexpectedly, and the grandmother cried in depths not known by the on-watchers at the time, but is now understood by her. We mothers, we sisters, we wives, we friends, we all, at some time face losses which leave us changed, that's all, just changed.

And sometimes she goes to keening. It is a comfort. It is a release perhaps only understood by the old ones before us. She may not have realized it at the time, but now she knows that she is not alone. The ancients are with her. Perhaps they are keening from another world in concert with her own sounds. Perhaps they are not there at all. She prefers to believe they are with her. All those gone before her must surely know how very lonely she is at times. She closes her eyes. She rocks in the chair, and she keens.

Cher Duncombe

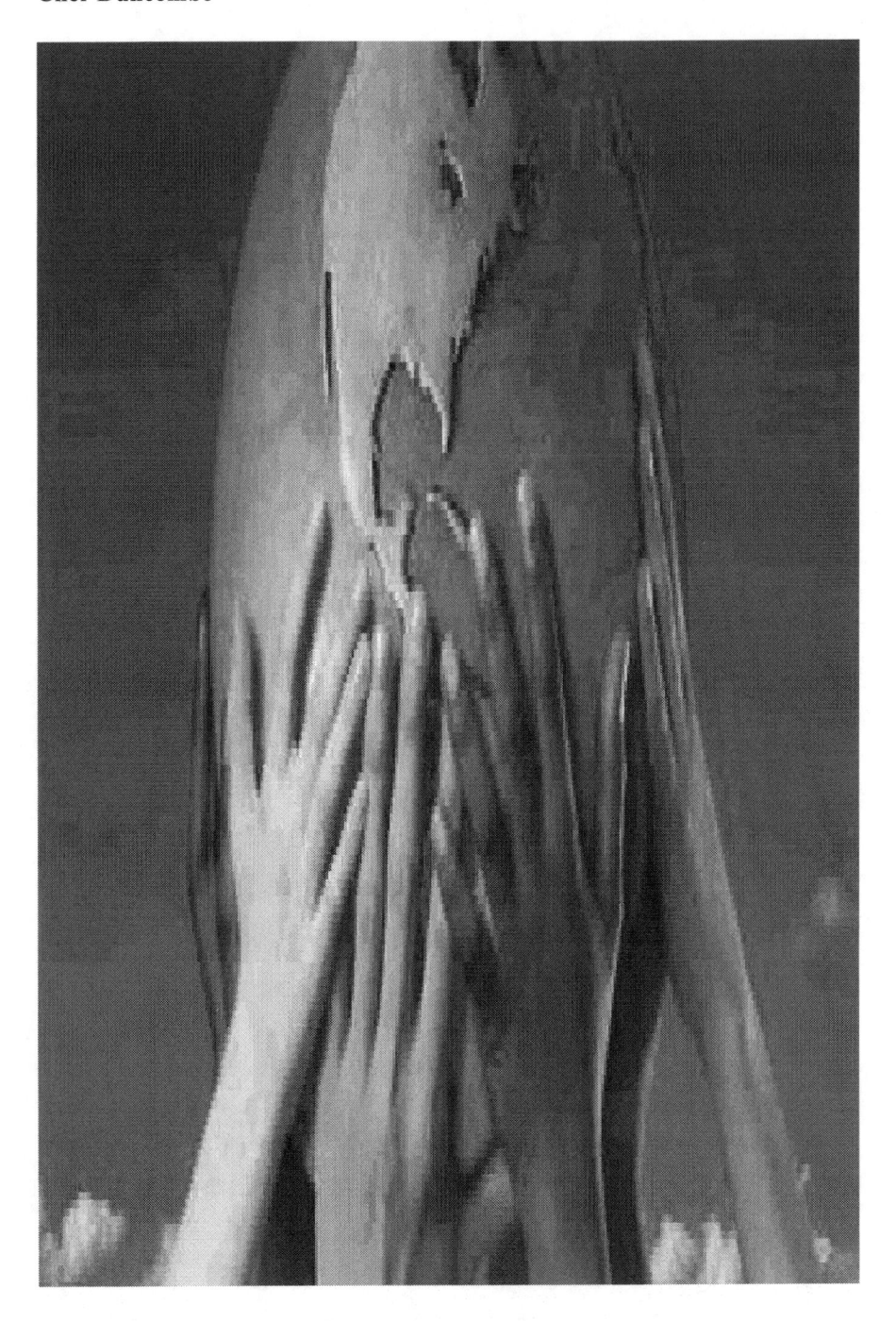

In a World Less Jaded

"The evil that men do lives after them; the good is oft interred with their bones."~~~William Shakespeare

There are days when I read the newspapers and watch cable news channels only to find myself sickened by depravity and despair. At times I find my mind seeking the fantasy of a world less jaded. In this world there are many issues that would become the ex-factors, deleted from my reality like a spelling error when I am typing. Control-Alt-Delete would be my defense of choice, an eraser for thoughts best not spoken or written.

In my world less jaded, there would be no white supremacists, no child predators; no subjugation of women; no politicians who sacrifice mankind at their whim; no hunger for those who need fed; no judgments upon well-meaning souls; no greed at the expense of integrity; no cliques that keep others out and keep themselves in; no stranger danger for children and adults alike, and no mandated supreme dogmatic religion that relegates non-followers to a hell on earth.

In my world less jaded there would be unconditional love for friends and family; there would be tolerance for those who color outside the lines; there would be more smiles and fewer tears; there would be forgiveness of grievances; there would be an enlightenment which acknowledges differences; there would be an embracing of values that are built on good intentions, and there would be no diminished capacity of importance for those who see through a different lens.

"You may say I'm a dreamer, but I'm not the only one," sang John Lennon many years ago. I am a self-admitted dreamer, but if this world keeps spinning into a deeper shade of jade, I would be one of the first to be put into a barbed-wire compound for dreaming the dreams of fools. And though I am a dreamer, why do I have more and more thoughts of needing a gun for protection? Why have I put a security system in my home? Why is isolation becoming more and more of a necessity?

I am my own dichotomy. The mistakes I have made will live after me. The good I have tried to do will be interred with my bones. Until I round the bend to the midnight of my existence, I will still dream of a world less jaded, for that dream is my sustenance. Perhaps one day I will see those dreams come to fruition. Until then, like so many others, I will set my security alarm at night and forego the prayers that lay me down to sleep eternally. Control-Alt-Delete.

Cher Duncombe

Shading The Truth

Hitting the Wall

There are times when a series of events collides into calamity. We all have had them. Dealing with them is another matter. I try to call upon faith when I'm at such low ebb, but my voice seems weak and failing, unable to reach the heights of higher powers. I read quotes from famous and not-so-famous people. They sound very profound. I leave the pages with more emptiness.

Life is hard. No one said it would be easy. Are we born with intuitive defense mechanisms which fail from overuse? Can the heart hurt so much over the course of time that it just gives up and gives out? I count the seconds, minutes, hours, in darkness and wait to see if my heart will just stop, and with it the pain.

Maybe I'm all wrong here; perhaps it is in the brain and not the heart at all. An aneurysm with a quick anvil would do the trick. Kevorkian. Where is he? I ponder whether anguish trumps physical pain enough to qualify for his services. Oh, it is all such belittling self-pity, is it not?

I have lived long enough to know that the pendulum will eventually swing the other way. But the anguish has grown weary of waiting for the morphine of light which may not find its way to me in this dark place. If I find my way to morning, then I am just meant "to be" like a passive verb. It is an answer. It is enough. Tomorrow I will be a passive verb. Perhaps the next day I will be an active verb.

Gandy Dancing On The Second FLoor

Cher Duncombe

Garett And Medical Marijuana

In the 1990's I worked as a social worker. Within our office there was a lot of healthy camaraderie. It arose out of a need to keep our energy from being depleted though helplessness. We heard many sad and wretched stories from our clients during the day, but we tried to give them as much help as possible within the bureaucratic system. This kind of work can be depressing. One is at a loss to "fix" people and that really was not our job. The hearts of my co-workers were huge and filled with empathy. Many of us had, at one time or another, fallen on hard times ourselves. The system is limited in its ability to adequately see that proper food, health care, and homes were provided to those in dire need. Numbers. It's all about numbers and cold hard facts. Through it all, the workers spoke during breaks or lunch of their own families, various plights we were facing, and this became an internal support group.

One of the social workers in our office was Garrett, known for the best lunches any wife packed for any man, ever. I was living in Pittsburgh, and if you know anything about the 'Burgh, you will understand how we salivated over Garrett's lunches of Isaly's chipped ham with mayo, lettuce, and tomatoes on the one and only, Mancini's bread! Garret had a smile that melted into his entire face and every day he offered us part of his lunch. He was a tall, skinny man and I guess we figured he needed as many calories as possible. Little did we know at that point how important those calories would become.

One day we were all gathered in the break room. Garrett was unusually quiet and looked solemn. We waited for him to speak. "I have pancreatic cancer," he said. A shiver went over the room. We all knew the prognosis. In the weeks and months that followed, Garrett underwent chemo. He had a wife and two teenage boys, but came to work almost every day so he could accrue more benefits for them when the end came. We doted on him with love. As thin as he had been, his weight seemed to drop so rapidly that soon, he was a walking bone structure with a sunken face. He was also cold. It was winter, hideous winter. I brought a space heater for his cubicle and a cozy afghan for his lap to keep him warm. His appetite was gone. No more Mancini bread sandwiches. He was drifting away from us.

One day he said to me, "Kiddo, can you get me some, you know…(he stumbled) pot? Some weed?" Why he asked me is a mystery, but I believe it was a matter of trust.

Marijuana was verboten, prohibited, against the law. But I knew people who knew people. I got some weed and baked the whole lot of it in a batch of brownies. I surreptitiously gave the large pan of goodies to him on a Friday afternoon. Monday morning he came into my cubicle and gave me the biggest bear hug I have ever had. He said that he and his wife had eaten all marijuana-laced brownies over the weekend. He had such an appetite, he said, and his wife had cooked for him the entire time. He also said it was the best he had felt physically in ages. Garrett was filled with gratitude, and I just wanted to magically instill him with that permanent feeling of euphoria. He had been suffering a long time.

Two months later, Garrett was in the hospital for the last time. His doctors prescribed medical marijuana for him during that stay. His wife later told us that the medical marijuana had eased his final days. We all took Garrett's death hard. He was a gentle man, a young man, a good man. And except for that one weekend and the pot-laced brownies, he had suffered hard. His wife would later tell us that she received a bill from the hospital for $700.00. She was charged for the medical marijuana even though the physician had prescribed it and the hospital had filled it.

I tell you this story to put a face to the need for medical marijuana. There is no shame in it. But I also take this a step further and ask, why isn't marijuana, weed, pot, legalized all over the country? It could be regulate, less anyone get weed that has been laced with angel dust, as I once had and ended up in a fetal position, unable to feel my left side for three hours. Some states are moving toward this. There will always be detractors like those during Prohibition. It is such nonsense. We are a callous, backward lot at times. Think about my friend Garrett the next time someone asks you whether medical marijuana should be legalized. The use of weed should not be a criminal offense. Not providing it for medical use should be criminal. Use your vote to voice your opinion. At the very least, medical marijuana should be legalized. Garrett would like that, Kiddo.

Cher Duncombe

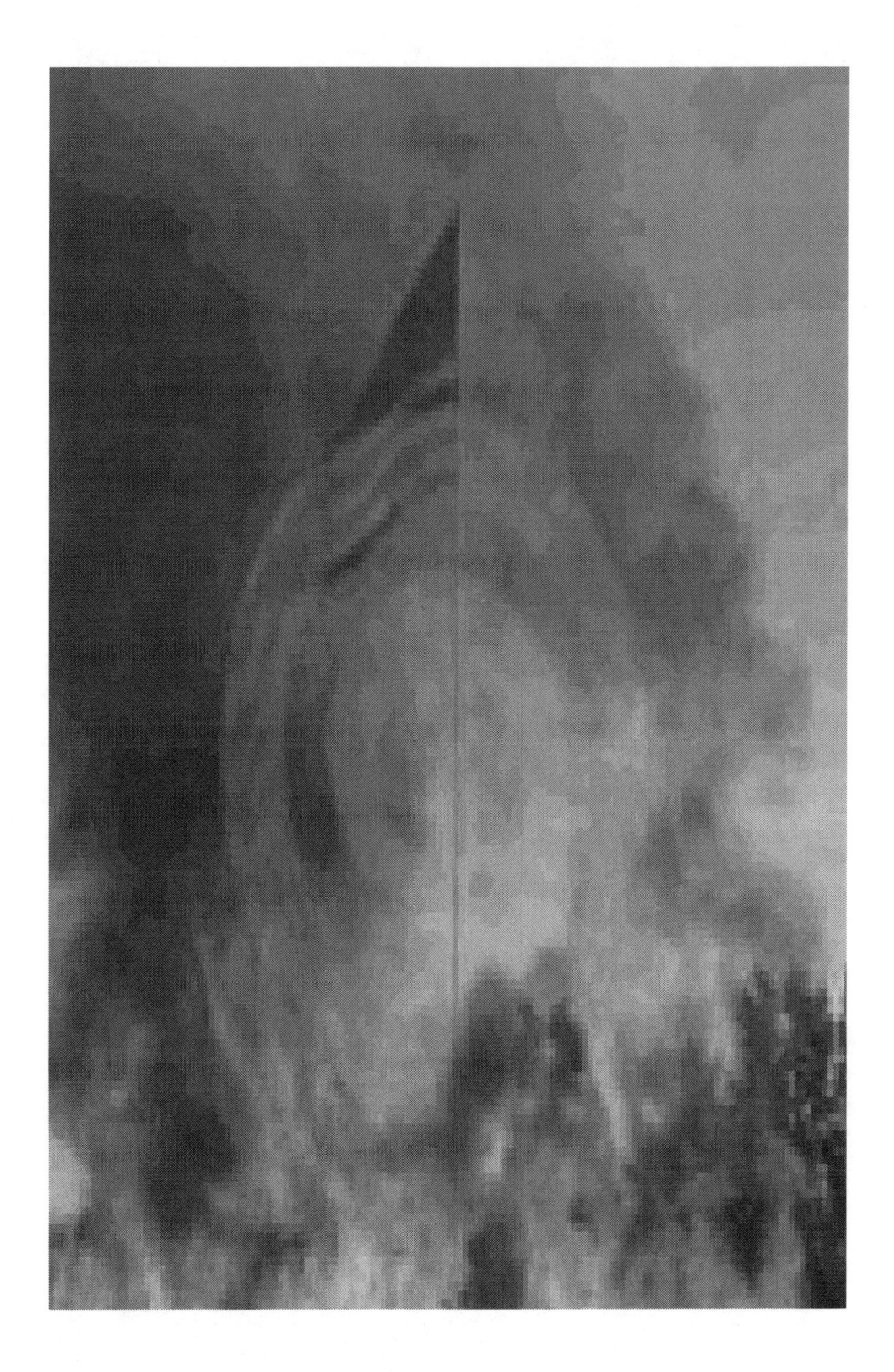

SAM AND A PTSD TUNNEL OF WAR

I made a friend some years ago whom I will never forget. I will call him Sam. He had been a Marine in Vietnam and suffers from Post-Traumatic Stress Disorder. When I met Sam, his conversations threw me back into the clutches of time that stirs a cauldron of emotions in me. Having come of age during the Sixties, I thought after decades had passed, that I had developed a perspective of that era which neither romanticized it nor intellectualized it. Somewhere in the middle was the truth as I had lived it, a college student looking for reality through an unfocused lens.

When I met Sam, I knew that whatever my perceptions had been, they now seemed irrelevant. Forget the music; forget the flowers; forget the clothes, and forget the political rhetoric from all sides. Sam had been there, in 'Nam, and in the depths of his psyche he remains there still.

I am ashamed to say that despite reading about PTSD, I had only viewed it from afar. Some issues in life are like that. Until you or someone close to you experiences trauma, your ability to fully empathize is somewhat hindered. My own psyche, in all honesty, did not want to get too close to Sam's reality. It is like knowing someone who has cancer and in the darkest part of your heart, you are glad it isn't you. But Sam has become my friend and since he relives his time in Vietnam through nightmares that surface through the day, he has taken me on a journey through the deep tunnel of his mind. I was a reluctant traveler. I will not share with you the visions and sounds Sam describes to me. I can only share with you my sight of a man suffering. If you don't want to see this accident, keep your car moving and avert your eyes.

My friend fights sleep every night so that he can stay on alert. In case. His sleep deprivation gives rise to voices and sounds. "Did you hear that?" The demons never rest and neither does Sam. He has a shoebox full of medications, and he faithfully counts them out every day. He was ordered, he said, to do this by the VA doctors. Ever obedient, he does as he was told. But the meds only dull him for a few hours. The visions are still there; they are just blurred. As the meds begin to wear off, Sam cocks his head, squints his eyes, and stays on watch. His visions are back full force before the next round of meds can be taken, and his fear and trembling begin again.

After Sam's wife died, Sam continued to raise his three boys to adulthood, but in truth, the boys took care of Sam in loving and nurturing ways that were beyond their years. Sam had a beautiful home built for his family and he calls it "the compound." It is structured, in Sam's mind, to keep his boys safe. He is considered severely disabled and cannot hold a job. But he has a genius IQ, and speaks with the soul of a poet with a meandering mind. I can follow his thread for a while, then he trails off into unknown territory. All I can do is listen. I stare at the paintings done by Sam on every wall in his home. None are done in muted tones but each holds a story that only Sam knows.

Sam makes my heart cry and I am helpless to still his pain. I see his glazed eyes and know that he is in a place and time far away. There are no arms long enough to reach him, to go into that dark tunnel and pull him back. He may forever live in that sorrow.

I don't know why certain people are put in our lives. Maybe I was meant to meet Sam so I could share this with you. I don't know. I am certain, though, that we must never avert our eyes and that we must never forget those who have served our country. Their journey was long and painful, and there are those who are still in battle.

Cher Duncombe

Dark Clover

Under the clover I will hide me today

Darkness descends here where I lay

Shroud of mist help me not breathe

Stay very still and then he will leave

Oh God where are you I almost forgot

That fear and foreboding, this is my lot

Gandy dance now and someone may hear

The voices of evil that scream in my ear

Be very still and perhaps you will see

The girl who lived in dark clover was me

Gandy Dancing On The Second FLoor

Trees and Clover

Cher Duncombe

Blind Politick

You blister my mind with your venom

And there are those who are unwitting

Accomplices

In the pandering parade of foolish clowns

Truth is the blindspot in your bloodsport

It is the frayed fringed edge of desperate

Denial

In loathing that which you began long ago

But it is not me whom you fear; it is your

Night terrors given life through disregard of

Sanctity

In the place that once held high its courtesans

Thoughts unwritten, deeds undone, languishing

In a purgatory created by fictional illusions of

Righteousness

Piety that brought down kings and wrought peril

Be you at peace even as the sod of earth shakes

For loud are the cries of the bewildered bastions

Loyal

Once when peace prevailed and harmony reigned

Cher Duncombe

A Man of Casual Words

He sat shoulder-slumped on the sidewalk as

I, primed for entrance to the chic boutique

Walked briskly for grazing evening wear

His eyes followed; he said Hello Ma'am and

I turned to meet his smile of warm cinnamon

In a gaze I took his measure, but walked inside

As the evening wear swung, hanger by hanger

No interest had I, since I knew he was out there

Alone, unkempt, wrapped in beaten-down jacket

And a hat of unknown variety, certainly not chic

I exited but dared to walk through a new door

Are you, were you, I asked as I stopped before him

Nam, said he, I'm so sorry said I holding his eyes

Then saw one stump of a leg, a casualty of a time

When flames burned in one place, flags in another

As I reached for my wallet, No, said he, No Ma'am

Thanks, I served you know, my country back then

And proud of it, you see, said in cinnamon smile

As he tilted his head up toward me, and I felt so

Small, so inadequate compared to his sincerity, to

The remnant of a leg lost for those who spat and sang

And chanted and disrespected the honor of a man with

Casual words and a cinnamon smile that haunt me still

Gandy Dancing On The Second FLoor

Cher Duncombe

Cape May

It calls to me in beckoning of sensual sand sounds

As waves billow forth and subside like a lover's hands

Again, again, in waves and surges beneath ocean torrents

That filter and foment in erotic urges of earthen libido

Until I am drenched in its morass of unquenching thirst

Morn peers subtly as I lie upon grains, so still with traces

Of the quest conquered in surrender to an iridescent tide

And somewhere a bagpipe is played far down the shore

By a silhouette of a man giving homage to the dawn in its

Breaking with hues that nullify the night and leave me aching

Cher Duncombe

Life on a Wire

Stranger things have happened than life on a wire

And reaching for truths that eclipse balance

Must all be in perfect order, universal in compliance

Or can there be dreams contemplated in flight fancy

A yearning for spells namelessly cast yet vivid in color

And who shall determine perception as reality

The curators of heart must seek tempo sublime

In the melancholy melody that enriches love

For then, only then will arrive the overflowing overture

As it opens the musical whimsy of entwining personas

In a fugue of symphonic and altered chords

Stranger things have happened than life on a wire

Cher Duncombe

In the Heart

There is emptiness here in the heart

Yet I wonder if there was ever more

Where does reality begin, fantasy end

Distance between then and now is vague

Was the fire warm or just remembered so

Longing lingers as a hunger unfulfilled

Was there passion, was there pretense

Somehow the answers matter not

For there is an emptiness here in the heart

The Blues

Dedicated to Gary Moore

April 4, 1952 to February 6, 2011

Irresistible God-chords in hues of sorrow

Blistered fingers and aching soul

Anguish plucked, raw and bleeding

Notes that spill like wine upon saints

And sinners, all of whom know that

Redemption comes only from the Blues

Cher Duncombe

Dream Cover

Just please hold me, Baby
In these hours of monsters
And faces I almost recognize
But fear...
Their names are near to my
Tagging though not quite yet
Through blurred vision, familiar
So close...
Wrap me in down to silence
Those voices speaking to me
With words of soul-bruises
In Hush...
And when you hear me cry
Know I'm not meant for here
Too frail, too fragile, to fall into
Their grasp...
Again not again not now not then

Still they haunt these hollows of
My psyche but never knew who
I was....

Cher Duncombe

The Appointment

In the shallow end of my pool resides would-be doctor

Beside him is ditsy receptionist, blonde with black roots

Not bad people, really, just inept at facts and facets of life

They smile ridiculous smiles devoid of truth and empathy

Automatons have more abilities than dolts with no shame

I feed them tea and biscuits at four, promptly on time

The way it should be when someone has thirst for help

And when their fingertips shrivel from too much chlorine

They are given towels to warm their vapid spirits, make them

Understand that even a patient can be kind, can listen with

Virtue, not disingenuous mumbles one must strain to hear

They may ask me questions and I may give succinct answers

Clearly understood without patronizing platitudes or clown-frowns

I shall release them one day when they too have pain from

Degenerative disc disease, beg for quality of life, plead for mercy

And stop those goddamn smirks

Cher Duncombe

Rooms

Rooms in My Life

These places, these scenes,

I count them over the course of time

Duly noting those rooms now empty,

Only dust or lint or an occasional

Scrap of paper or theater ticket stub.

I close thoughts quickly, lest the past

Envelop me in a cloak of ragged edge.

Moving into sanctity of current rooms,

I find burning candles, and new photos,

Faces imprinted in my imagery to light

My way as I meander through memories

Dark and light.

 And the scent of surrender

Both entices and forebodes excursions to

Be taken and new rooms to be decorated

In shades of burnt orange and earthy green,

Cher Duncombe

And colors welcoming through windows

Not opened before, before, when I was hidden

In rooms with no doors nor glistening light,

And unearthly echoes of dare me knots

Tied to a place and to rooms I shall visit

No more.

The Butterfly

I thought of you a little less today

Threads of my being entwined in repair

Tears of my soul stood still on my cheek

But the sound of your voice could not be hushed

Words you spoke both loving and leaving

Will linger through my tomorrows

Somewhere I will see you, butterfly in hand

And my heart will know that once it was me

I thought of you a little less today

Cher Duncombe

The Mentor

I did not know his name but he was a catalyst

A new blogger was I, exploring space clouds

Writing thoughts of politics, poetry, platitudes

Into a vast arena I ventured, unsure, hesitating

Wanting only to write yet needing to be part of

Who would care who would read did it matter

Surprise came in a message from beyond keys

You have no avatar!

What is an avatar?

And so it went with this person unidentified

Known only as Topmaker an intriguing name

As time went on he offered his hand in help

I thought it was he or was it she, Topmaker

So much knowledge shared, kindness given

And when I asked to pay the answer was this

Pay it forward!

Pay it forward?

No answer given but an iron bond was forged

In years that followed like a swiftly passing train

Topmaker taught me code, designed my blog, more

More than anything this invisible person became

My trusted friend, my mentor, my encourager, when

Stress overwhelmed and doubts completely nagged

I can't!

Yes you can!

One day the answer to a long lasting question arrived

My name is Mohammad he said with wary confidence

And here was my friend trusting me, waiting, curious

Perhaps even cautious from perhaps unwarranted fear

My heart leapt at the knowing, mind raced with gratitude

I knew him as a teacher possessing intellect grace sacrifice

You are my gift!

You are my gift!

In all my days remaining on this earth in time, space and clouds

This mentor shall be endeared always, held closely in mind

In heart in knowledge of how we learn and forge bonds in trust

Paying it forward through unfettered kindness in world so hugely

Callous and inopportune with judgments and superficial values

His name is Mohammad, my valued friend loved in Godly spirit

Forever?

Forever!

Women in Courage

They would not let us vote
We did
They put us on the back of the bus
We moved
They wanted our minds numb
We worked
They paid us less
We fought
They abused and battered us
We left
They want us quiet
We speak
They take our clinics
We rally
They speak in denigrations
We scoff
Again, again, again they shun us
We stand
Brave
Intelligent
Strong
Feminine
Women
Speaking
Together
United
Strong
Free

Cher Duncombe

Where Are You

Sanity 101

A visit was made to the Freudian scholar

He, in Chesterfield coat and John Lennon glasses

I, in suspended animation

Behind the mahogany desk he sat

Waving his hand toward a wooden chair

Isolated in the center of the room

A test, to be sure, should I move that chair

Sanity determined by positioning

Daunted by the task I floated through windows

And did not find myself that day

Cher Duncombe

The Passenger

In the cable car she rode alone observing

Not the city before her but something near

Cast in gold shadows and light fading upon

The vacant seats

Yet a presence was known and bidding her to

Dark thoughts and portends of what may come

As the car bumped and groaned upon the rails

Halting then swaying

Her thoughts toward present, past, future and

The certainty of the uncertain, fairness of unfair

Then peace upon her came as she knew that this

Presence was divine

Not evil, and would determine her ride, her endpoint

Cher Duncombe

So she gazed upon the city she had loved for so long

And again beheld its beauty and the life she had lived

Within its arms

Gandy Dancing On The Second FLoor

Cher Duncombe

Not Quite

Dedicated to My Husband, Richard

It was a carefree calliope of time in which he took her on a journey
Through fields, and to the sea, and on open roads to wild
Wanderings of laughter and music and moonlight madness
As she tossed back her hair and the wind carried them like a sail
They were children and grown-ups all in one sweep of time
But moon tides came and wanton wind currents changed course
Steering them into the times of restlessness and pretensions
Still they yearned to go back to the fields, open road, and the sea
Their journey had ended for a while as dark stars beckoned them in
A bidding of come hither and they knew that no matter how life had
Held them in a grasp of desolation, despair and heart-wrenching pain
Their journey would continue in a free spirit of love-always markers
Which told them, not quite, not quite, is your journey complete
For her hair was tossed back in a sail and the

words he spoke were
Melodies by which they would live their lives
in torrents and currents
On a journey that never quite ended through
an eternal quest in love

Cher Duncombe

Secrets

You speak to me in evenly measured tones

Hiding a cacophony of thoughts

I stretch my heart to grasp your essence

But you move in twilight eluding me

There are secrets in these moments, shadows and ghosts entwine

I smile, giving you coffee in a blue cup

And hope you don't notice my trembling hand

You are vague and I am raw

I light a cigarette and inhale deeply

There are secrets in these moments, shadows and ghosts entwine

Gandy Dancing On The Second FLoor

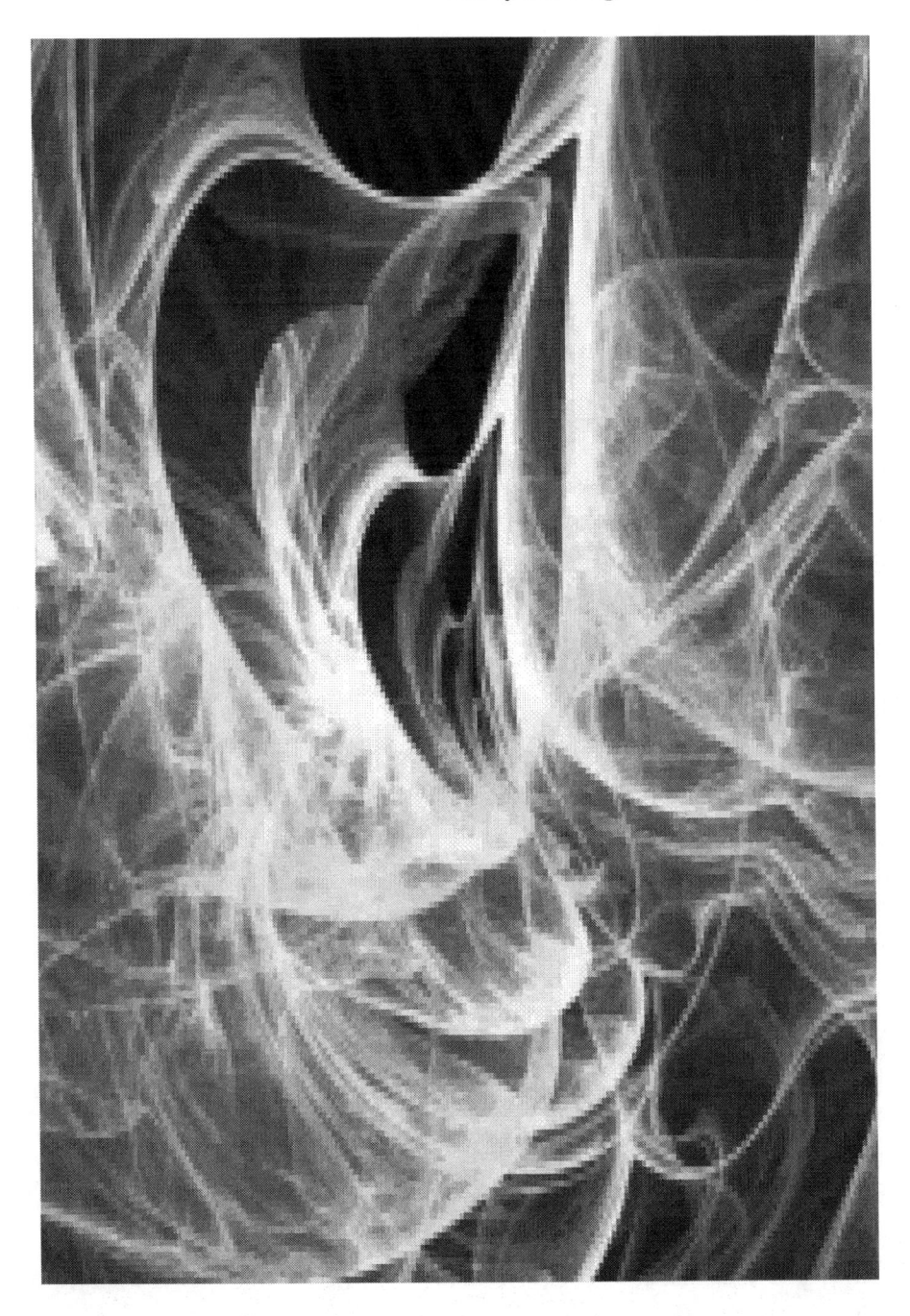

Cher Duncombe

Love in Nourishment and Toxins

In a surreal sense it is intangibles that multiply in a DNA dance of microbes and variables
Invisible until you see that smile, or eyes that lock with yours in a symbiotic gaze

It warms something called the heart but surely emanates from the mind in psychic allure
Unless of course you are a man and it begins in physicality, postulates in fantasy

That begets
    Beguiles
    Begs then bemoans

As she purrs
    Promises
    Prompts and probes

Bodies meld in temporal tumult
    Taunting
    Tasting and tormenting

For minutes, for days, for months, for years...for now, for now alone it is harmony with haste, a mixture of antidotes, cures for the ailments, salve for the aches, blinding of past

Cher Duncombe

Give to me; take from me; drink of my sweat, and slide upon the slopes and whisper your Wails while together we forget in the anesthesia of endorphins that satiate our thirst

In these moments of lavish
      Lusting
      Lingering and languishing

While fools frolic in abandon not knowing what is nourishing and what is toxic and when
To stay and when to leave before the sun rises or sets upon love that lost its virgin vortex

Of Forests and Oceans

Tread softly into the forest so deep

In stillness seek solace of nature to keep

Hold out your hand, touch gently the leaves

Of trees rooted in time and space that now grieves

Abandoned by mortals in selfish life passage

Have we forgotten their counsel and message

Tend to this earth and with it your soul

Reflect on these gifts and be yourself whole

For oceans and wildlife the willow does weep

And errant the gestures of man in his sweep

Tend to my sister, the forest does groan

She's aching and breaking and now she does moan

How bonded they are, these siblings of earth

Now do they cry in fear of stillbirth

Cher Duncombe

Unraveling God

To those upon whom words fall silently

Through hungry souls yearning for solace

For others whose long rote memories

Kept them seeking the fullness of that

Once taught, once believed, once cherished

In fullness of faith of things believed, not seen

What has been learned in grievous sins, cast

In wages of death and heartbreak

Is that their eyes were on men of cloth unraveling

When in depth of fact, faith and prophecy,

They should have remained on God

Gandy Dancing On The Second FLoor

Cher Duncombe

Looking Through Photos

This is the one, my first love

I hear no trumpets touting

A dirge, perhaps, but no trumpets

In college we met, you see

In college we married, you know

So happy, so young, so innocent

In the naiveté of life's unkindness.

It knocked on our door uninvited

Like a portend of grief undeserved

Something happened

Something unfair

His laughter became fear

His thoughts lost in a maze

Faltering

Flailing

Floundering

Communists in the TV

Communists, I asked

Everywhere, he answered

His essence evaporated

Leaving only the physical shell, now distorted

Riding home from the diagnosis, alone I was,

And dressed in sackcloth and ashes while

Wailing at God up above, how could you

He is so good

He loved you

And you gave him this, but why

Paranoid

Schizophrenia

No cure

No hope

But one day, many years later

He danced at our son's wedding

And in the corner with no one to see

I cried

Cher Duncombe

Night Driving

Halogen headlights in a Stephen King haze
Face me as I drive through the rainy night
A caramel macchiato is my only passenger
It lets me sip some insipid thoughts
Without feeling maudlin or ecstatic, just free

My eyes blink with the windshield blades as rain
Pellets the glass and tries my last nerve in fog
The rain is okay, really, has an undercurrent beat
iPod plugged to shuffle, check, Gary Moore's Blues
I love the rhythmic movement of car and melodies

I sound pretty good, actually, in this acoustic chamber There's no audience but I think about Broadway or Some piano bar where I could have sung sultry songs In the days when cigarette smoke would have replaced fog And my hair was long and flowing down my back

I need to thaw chicken for dinner tomorrow but where's That recipe I saved for special guests and impressive dining? Doesn't matter; improvising works; linen napkins, white wine Savory spices, slow cooking, and

**flowers on the table Amazing how driving
clears my mind and...the fog is lifting**

Cher Duncombe

Dreams In Moonlight

In dark persuasion does moonlight fall

Yielding to rays of a bygone sun

Secrets lie solemn in shadows of night

Fear strikes hard with a hastening pulse

Wicked, merciless, dreams ravage these hours

Oust from the blackness sins of my past

Send light and roses and promise of redemption

Cher Duncombe

In a Shell

It is a quiet place with no pain
Without doors
In the silence of night-reckoning
Without sound
I sit in this shell pulled 'round
Without wisdom
In tokens taken from none
Without owing
It taunts me to stay comatose
Without feeling
In state of invisible living
Without sight
I dwell in contemplation
Without thought
In the knowing of some
Without

In Limbo

An easy retreat, this walkabout in existence

Strolling in limbo looking for signs of

Direction, uncertain, unyielding, unstopping

Not moving, no feeling, no pain, no joy, no care

Empty. Silent. Safe. Apathy. Ambivalence.

Exhausting sublimation

Cher Duncombe

A Boomer's Lament

This one walked with me each day
On a curling path to school
Children we were in flannel innocence
Chatting, strolling, as leaves spun
In a dervish of quickened time and
A slow burning truth took him to war
Daisy chains, Dylan, banter and brocade
Did little to mask the loss of
Sweet talks under street lights
Dimmed by ashes of far away fires while
A slow burning truth melted our dreams

Cher Duncombe

In Melancholy

Melancholy wraps itself around me

Deceptive in its warmth and allure

Like notes in a song I once heard

That gave me Blues for my blues

As I push against the pillow of sad

My strength diminishes and I relent

Allowing it to envelop me in tears

Which no one can see with earthly eyes

Perhaps tomorrow shall be

Perhaps I shall be

Perhaps I shall do

And perhaps not

Swimming in a Quagmire

Too much exertion in trying to grasp

An essence so deeply rooted in elusive

Contractions and expansions with weight

So deep that it pulls me limb by limb and

As I fight against it my body still, even now

Yearns for the coupling, the entwining, the joy

Of absolute abandon, and sensual torrents in the

Muddied mind of your saddened, dark being

Cher Duncombe

Stained Words

Too many words given credence

Too many minds empty, absorbing

And what is defined as truth

Becomes defiled in violence

Erupting through volcanic thoughts

Spewing ash in the form of bullets

Taking lives in unjustified and vulgar

Attempts at recognition and assertions

Of power through I AM, the id of

Idiosyncrasy and Ideology, simple pleasures

Of indoctrination that spill blood, leaving

The stains of ruination and grief

Quiet Alignment

In situations dark and brooding

Forces unite in bonded strength

If only for quixotic moments

That re-arrange an estranged

Universe in small pockets

And there is a quiet alignment

In which dark and light converge

Melding into harmony and grace

If only for those ticks of time

When clocks may slow a hastening

World from its mad frenzy and

Give it unbridled joy in nanoseconds

Cher Duncombe

The Market

It was an odd day at the market

Crowded with assorted people

Rudely crashing carts in aisles

And caring not about brusque bumps

Nor the toppling of cans which rolled

Carelessly to be stumbled upon as

Accidents about to happen

Undaunted she tripped unwittingly not

Finding what she truly needed and feeling

Like a bruised peach returned to the bin

Carelessly tossed about then landing in a

Stack of the shocked and awed while being

Placed with damaged dented cans like

Premeditated murder of spirit

In a sand of time she heard a soft whisper

A comforting sound in the market of

Hidden treasures where carts are brusque

She turned, seeing only his eyes but what

Color are they, and why is he in this bin

He does not appear bruised so it must be

Misappropriation of value

But he spoke to her in words of sweet

Kindness and told her of healing in the market

His words were as compelling as his mysterious

Eyes and he looked softly upon her bruise

He offered her wisdom and friendship now found

In the market of clanging carts, and as she saw his dents

He became a Renoir

One day she will return again to the market

She will gaze upon the Renoir which few can see

And she will know the layers of paint and brush strokes

That marks this, especially this, as a complete

Treasure to behold amidst brusque carts

On a good day in the market when friendship is

Whispered from an artist's soul

Quiver of Time

In a quiver of time she was transported

From girl to woman and placed in a tea cup
To be sipped with only sugar, no lemon

Those who thought they knew her
Were deluded by the actress in her role
Her eyes were cast downward as some spoke
While she listened to words blurred but acerbic

What she found in this theatre of the absurd
Were scripts not meant for her, a miscast of roles
She was required to be bold, no kerchief for tears
No stage right, nor stage left, no director waving arm

And in a quiver of time she placed the script in a kettle
To brew the leaves of their bitter flavor
For she would drink only tea with sugar, no lemon

Cher Duncombe

Act Two or Ten

Act Two or Ten

There are times when it seems quite natural
These acts of reconciliation or acts of contrition
Just for being
In total disdain she discards mimicking mirrors
In sudden impulse she shreds photos of evidence
That she survived
Sometimes she places her paintings toward walls
Away from sight as if to dismember her mind-body
From all life
She calls it disappearing herself and does so casually
As though she has penanced without committing sin
While incense wafts
In darkened chambers that echo cries of not long ago
Through yesterdays when she was battered till bled
And no one heard
Mother, father, thieves of soul, all gone now and yet
She cannot banish their words, their scars, soul-bruises
Lingering psychic torment
so

Cher Duncombe

**she
disappears
herself
Into an invisible shadow person who cannot
be harmed
By those supposed to care but know not the
juxtaposition
Of love pains**

Gandy Dancing On The Second FLoor

Cher Duncombe

Cave Dweller

It lives in recesses of dark corners and that's where I like to keep it.
Light-deprived, starved by my ignoring, it may raise its voice and
Scream
Not wanting my happiness, willing to devour, it sits like Gollum
Rubbing hands onto my psyche showing visions I have hidden
Scream
With its might and against my waning will, preservation of self,
Undetected devil inside cave, bat-memories caught in silken webs
Scream
Triggers are many. A shot from a gun. A suicide watch. A photograph.
A picturesque day. A taste of Wild Turkey. A travel guide to Atlanta.
Scream
It waits for the day when the sound is audible and laughter turns my reality
Upside down into hysterical blindness of what is truth and what happened
Scream
One day, though you will not hear me, I will over-ride this beast that bludgeons

**And bitch-slap it to infinity where it belongs,
again in shadows, invisible, dead,
Lying at the bottom of the cave and covered
in concrete when I win and say
Shut the fuck up**

Cher Duncombe

It Was 9/11

Smoke and fire swirled and flamed mixing gray with orange

Bodies dropped in leaps of despair, leaving us to gasp and sob

People ash-covered, shock-filled, roaming like zombies with

Why? What? Who? How?

New York sent their Brave, their Selfless to Search, to Rescue, to Comfort,

To Die in fallen floors as Towers toppled upon them without mercy

Firemen, Police Officers, Emergency Teams and Citizens unknown

Sought to save remnants of life in charred legs, torsos, fingers snapped

Plundered by aggravating assault, the innocents

In Shanksville the bold lay strewn in Fields of green now splattered in red

And the dead became our heroes, our patriots, our own, the triumphant

Unspeakable thought, our Pentagon hit as more died this sunny morning

Turned dark with danger, desperation, disbelief, disembodiment

Why? What? Who? How?

Incomprehensible ramblings in notes of fear and panic in this Land of

Free, Brave, Bold, Confused

And as I drove ninety miles office to home, Flags appeared along roads

But doors closed and silence hung like an eerie mantra of prayer rising

To God, Bless America, while my eyes blurred in hues of red, white, and blue

Cher Duncombe

Folded Hands

She folded her hands and said that's it

She folded her hands in prayer of save me

A dichotomy of conflicted thoughts

And wretched emotions churning

She folded her hands and listened for

She folded her hands and waited for

But stillness surrounded her

And the night seemed to envelop

She folded her hands fingers clasped

She folded her hands fingers undone

The phone rang and she listened

The answers had arrived, so sorrowful

She folded her hands and closed her eyes

She folded her hands saying take me home

It is time.

Cher Duncombe

The Counting

The cobblestone street on which I once lived

Has today been paved with modern mix asphalt

Too bad really, my yellow brick road

Has been depleted of its charming path

And the stained glass windows of my house that

Had beamed light in hues of rainbow blushes

Now replaced by eco-friendly panes of

Glass tinted to hold rays in, colors out

The cherry Quansan planted by me with care

Has been left unattended and abandoned as

Its shape withers from wanton winter storms

I count the ways we are alike, the house and I

My paths have changed, coursed in new direction

Taking me to untrodden roads with no cobblestones

And my windows are tinted as colors stay within

Lest someone peer inside and know I am as fragile

As the stained glass windows from my former home

And like the Quansan winter storms have battered

While I go hither into nights of fierce cold

Through memories of why's and wherefore's

Wolfe said I can't go home again, but I can count

The ways of life's changes and ponder lost cobblestones

Gandy Dancing On The Second FLoor

Cher Duncombe

Contessa

Tired hands dusting a floured apron

Dinners wrapped in flavors of love

Voices in surround sound nurturing

As we slip into Contessa's safehouse

She hovers, large in her smallness

Family anointed by her grace

Broken English the text of life

She harbors secrets we have yet to learn

White hair a crowning halo

Our Contessa dusting her floured apron

Cher Duncombe

The Artist

Needing grace in the morning light

A tender artist seeks mercy

Thorny roses prod at his soul

While memories bleed into pain

Vagrant of death hovers above

Tears of his Father now flow

Agony of ages brew in his mind

As demons call in dark whispers

He stands in still, shallow waters

And prays for grace in a mourning light

Cher Duncombe

A Day in September

This is the day I remember

Out of all the days in our lives

It was this one in September

You made a decision to end

All the rippled ribbons of love

My heart no longer could mend

And on this day in September

The sound of your gun still shatters

My hope for peace surrenders

In shadows, my brother, you ended

And today nothing else matters

For this is the day I remember

Gandy Dancing On The Second FLoor

Lilac Wall

Cher Duncombe

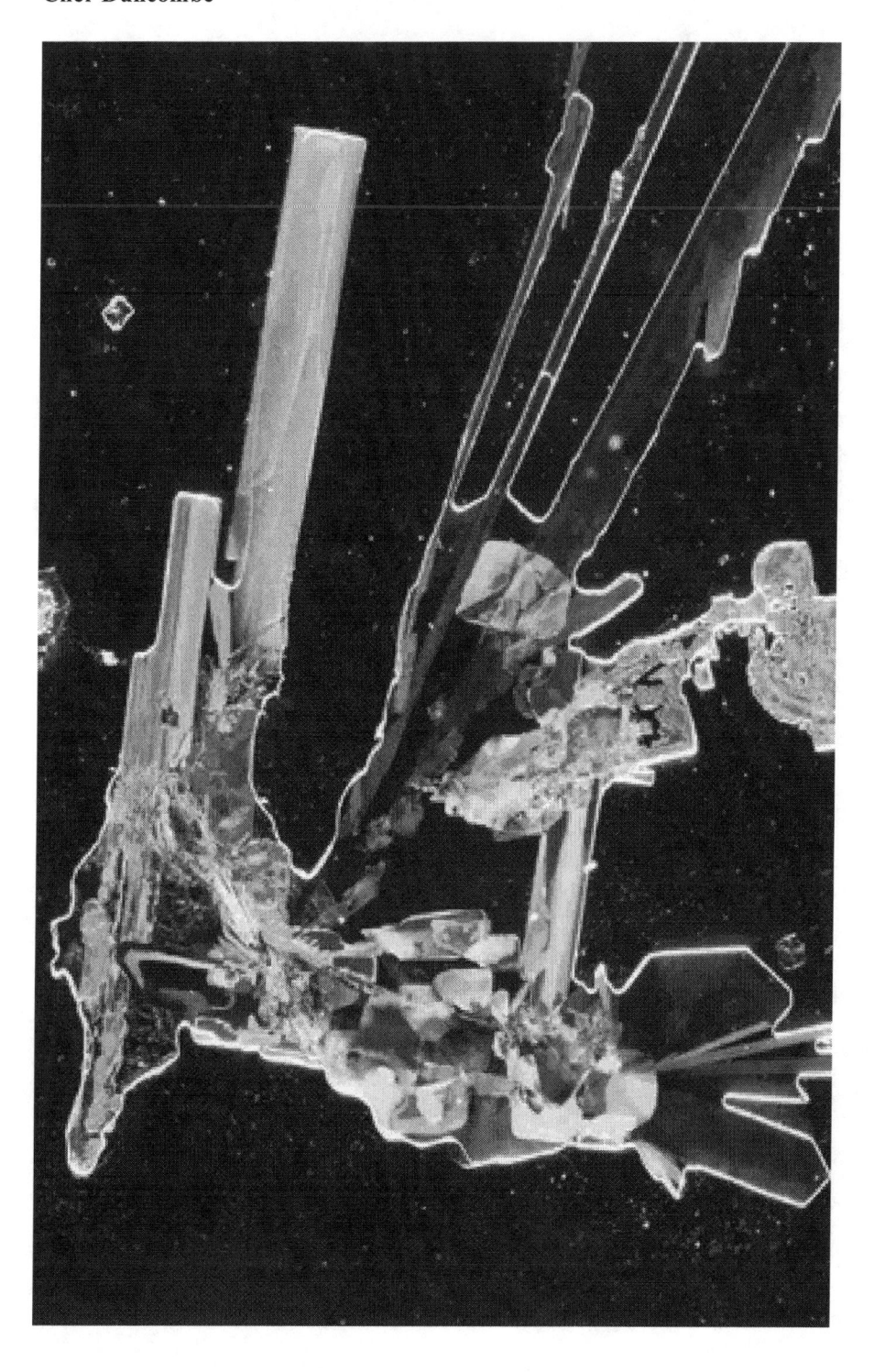

Raw

Feeling raw tonight

Like shards of glass

Are glazing my body

Heart, mind, and soul

Visions still too clear

Blood-spattered woods

Leaves stained by torment

Grass where his feet had

Ambled, now flat where

He lay moving no more

The gun wicked willing

Partner in self-inflicted

Crime in which I and we

Are now imprisoned by

His impetuous search for

Subsidence of pain

Cher Duncombe

And torn pleas for

Mercy

End

Peace

Love

Stay

Go

Gone

Now

And I and we are
Raw in endlessness of

Pain

Ache

Anger

Tears

Terror

Memories

Madness

Here

Cher Duncombe

The Codicil

It was your idea to draw up legal Wills, wretched documents

These ideas of what goes to whom and why and when

First, for our mother and given her illness, it seemed right.

She was already in a nether world, not knowing you nor me

But being a girl as in her youth, innocent, delicate, with a

Smile that washed away all the pain we knew was peeling her

Away from this delicate foothold in the present, knowing

Only days of long ago in a time before when pain did not exist

And the loss of her beauty had not begun and now she, too, was

Slipping away

Then came your notion, a trickery, a deceit, a foul ball

In the game of softball I had watched you play as a boy

When you rounded the bases and slid into home

So sure, I had said, draw up the papers for you and me

Sign here, here, and here, you said with casual cunning

I would be Trustee for your girls, the ones you lived for

And you would be Trustee for my kids, trust being the word

Of note since you were the only one to whom I gave mine

Through all the years of laughter, heartaches confided, and bonds

Sealed forever

I tucked away copies in a drawer of my oak desk, once owned by

A famous man and now, a treasured antique that held only one

Document of legal importance, signed by you, by me, and hidden

Then you boarded the plane to Atlanta and I waved as I always did,

Though too small for you to see once lifted from the runway into

Clouds like the ones we deciphered as children and had seen silly

Pictures or paintings from God's hands that had designed these images

For us to gaze upon when the world seemed solemn and without Grace

Or comfort to children who lived in fear moment to moment in secrecy

Just us

And one day, some months later, and after our mother had sailed

I was having dinner at the Rusty Nail, that quaint little place where we

Had dined and had spoken of ordinary things in extraordinary ways,

From the table in the back where the lights were more dim but your smile

Warm in the knowing that you were my only constant, the one who knew

All that was unknowable to anyone but us,
and in unconditional love we had

Spoken of the past, of survival, of today, of
tomorrows, of plans, of future...

My daughter entered with a flushed face
saying come home now, Mum

And from her visage, I knew. I knew. You
had an unwritten codicil in my desk

I, Trustee

Cher Duncombe has a Bachelor of Science degree in Secondary Education. She has taught English and Speech in high schools, but left teaching so she could pursue her passion for social work. Her career entailed working for several agencies, and her love was in being a community liaison. Later Cher Duncombe was hired as an Investigator for the Pennsylvania Office of Inspector General. Upon retiring from that career, Cher opened her own Private Investigations company.

Cher Duncombe resides in Florida with her husband Richard. She is also an artist. In Cher's words, "What I cannot speak, I write. What I cannot write, I paint."

Gandy Dancing On The Second FLoor

Cher Duncombe

Made in the USA
Columbia, SC
24 June 2025